SINFULLY SEDUCTIVE SWEETNESS

BY
AIYSHA SWALLOWGREN

ISBN: 978-0-9984840-8-2
First Printing July 2022
Printed in United States of America

Contents

ACCEPT

Love is being able to accept
Someone where they are at and forget
Any and all notions of being perfect
The two of us continue to deeply connect
By choosing love and to reflect
Kindly the parts of ourselves that are imperfect
We bravely choose to accept
Each other and we rarely expect
Anything but always there is respect
We are bold, brave, and very direct
We always have the right to object
Our relationship deepens the more we accept

AMAZING

You are beyond absolutely amazing
I feel compelled to start praising
You like maybe you have been praying
For appreciation and you deserve playing
With light I am gently bathing
Your soul and you are feeling amazing
New pleasurable sensations I am creating
You are fiery hot melting saying you are making
Me absolutely glow, you're energy is so invigorating
Your beauty is endlessly fascinating
You are beyond beautiful, so captivating
You make me want to keep raving
That I'm your biggest fan but what would be truly amazing
Is if you saw what I see there's an entertaining
Thought have I told you that you are breathtaking
Your body is so tone like all you do is training
I hope this brings you tears of joy hope it starts raining
Down blessings on you until you start shaking
Does this excite you what I am saying
Does this make you redefine amazing?

∞

Amazing 1

Growth and change are amazing
She appreciates positive phrasing
Also when the politeness bar keeps raising
She enjoys when he starts praising
Her mind and insights, she's pretty amazing
Herself looking at her is like stargazing
His careful listening and behaving
Like he's never experienced such a craving
Really got her going; he's slowly bathing
Her in sunshine with his complimentary raving
He says you're the best but I'm not saving
You for last as their minds start embracing
Oh the intellectual stimulation is amazing

Amplify

That feeling of turned on could we possibly amplify
That and bring even more colors to your eyes
Hate you leaving, love watching you walk goodbye
If you were a tree, you would be a bonsai
Here come the rain across the sky
You are a magnificent rainbow and I try
My very best to help you get really high
Oh I wonder if I could touch your thigh
I wonder if perhaps she would reply
Higher, put your hand really high
I bet you taste like sweet cherry pie
Two light beings start to unify
You say sir act like you work for the FBI
Inspect my female body I'll just lie
Back and you keep making me so not dry
With my words your body starts to electrify
Her brain goes from caterpillar to a butterfly
I want to turn you on then really amplify
That feeling and now let's magnify
That feeling more and more let's try
To get beyond turned on, let's amplify

∞

ARTISTIC

A toast for passion and inspiring artistic
Creation dear I hope to make you feel optimistic
Give you pleasure making your body go ballistic
Let me worship you fully in the most holistic
Manner giving you pleasure is spiritualistic
Allow me to share light, the most idealistic
Things like it's impossible for me to pick your best characteristic
Do you enjoy vulnerable men that embody altruistic
Cause your being makes me feel extra artistic

BATHING

Today in light I am totally bathing
You with the observation that you are beyond amazing
You deserve sincere, heartfelt praising
Your pleasure and acceptance keep raising
Let's make more light and keep making
Each other feel wonderful things all I'm saying
Is I want our brains and souls to be mating
Like let me write the most engaging
Things that set your soul blazing
Let me write things that get your heart racing
Let's keep growing, let's keep changing
For the better I have an insatiable craving
For your mind, for us to mentally start embracing
I have this to say and I'm not playing
How does it get sexier than you bathing?

∞

BEAUTIFULLY

I love speaking with love truthfully
You inspire me to think more beautifully
Between us the fun and laughter usually
Never stops together we experience unity
Together we experience a beautiful opportunity
To experience a whole year of jubilee
We raise the vibration in our community
People see us in bliss and how unusually
We express love, our art shines beautifully

BEYOND

Oh I'm so scared it's beyond
Terrifying I've avoided anger for so long
How can I move past they are wrong
How can I use this to make a love phenomenon
Would you help me move beyond
Anger and triumphantly burst into song
It's a similar path we are moving along
I feel like a sketch pad and you're a crayon
Would you draw me out and not prolong
The pain if you bravely gaze upon
My shadow I believe we can get beyond

Beyond Amazing

I know how to take her beyond amazing
With the most sincere praising
Her spirits and future keep raising
With sincere compliments I keep bathing
Her and she feels beyond amazing
She shows me the beauty of waiting
I know her deepest cravings
She wants to be loved without explaining
She's a wild cat and I'd never try taming
Her nothing gets her hotter than when I keep saying
You dear are truly stunning, beyond amazing
As I whisper you are absolutely breathtaking
I don't think I'll ever stop raving
About your beauty, you're beyond amazing

Black and White

I never believed in love at first sight
You make traffic stop like a stoplight
Woman I love you wearing black and white
You just being is able to ignite
Such passion and my brain fills with excite
To think of how to tell you how you delight
My senses and definitely my eyesight
Let's consciously make light
In the darkness we'll be the flashlights
What happens when beauty and consciousness unite
Let's ascend to the heavens, let's make skylight
Let our souls glow so big and bright
That we can be seen in space like a satellite
In the darkness we'll be the lone candlelight
We are changing the world from black to white

Blessing

Today a note about what a difference, what a blessing
You are how you've changed my stressing
Out into an opportunity to stop wrestling
With my demons all my pain and fear I'm letting
Go the lessons I'll never be forgetting
You made me stop searching for ways to be impressing
I am reminded of the true meaning of treasure, my greatest blessing
Is you opened my heart and mind to new forms of expressing
Love towards myself I started investing
In my health and things have been getting
Better and better I finally have been resting
In my dreams I have been constantly manifesting
You are truly my most cherished blessing

∞

Bone

Her heartbeat was irregular, it hurt to the bone
I whisper friends you will never be alone
She said it feels like my heart is stone
I sing in the most special tone
You're the most beautiful she reads her phone
My words send shivers down her backbone
She said this type of pleasure is unknown
She said I couldn't help but moan
You bring healing down to my bones
You let me fly free and never try to own
Me your sweetness is the sexiest cologne
What I give her is more valuable than any gemstone
When her heart feels like it's being hit by hailstones
I cover her in kisses licking her hipbone
I whisper look how much you have grown
With you I know more than I've ever know
More pleasure, more desire, she quietly groans
Let's have you sit on the most scared throne
She makes a wish and snaps the wishbone
Healing down to your very bone

BUTTER

You are hot toast and I am butter
Bringing you so much pleasure you forget what it is to suffer
Fanning the flames more sweetness please so here's another
Poem to help you magnificent creature discover
New levels of pleasure I desire to make you shudder
From pleasure as you gaze upon me in wonder
I wonder if I can make you taste colors
Could I do something no other lover
Has done before your body is a machine gun and I'm the gunner
Firing on all cylinders your body is tone like a runner
You have been running through my mind you are my favorite upper
Like butterfly wings my light kisses lightly flutter
All over your body and mind until you can barely utter
Oh sir you are making me melt everywhere like butter
I want to make you feel so good you start to stutter
Oh sir, sir I swear you're an undercover
Devil I'm as hard as a rock and you're a stonecutter
Meaning you're a massive diamond, let my fingers hover
Lightly on your brain melting like butter

∞

BUTTERFLIES

Spirit ignite magnetic butterflies
Silence my ego, let blessings multiply
Time for my spirit to fly
Goodbye caterpillar, hello beautiful butterflies
I prayed fervently spirit make me wise
Spirit said let's give these ladies butterflies
Let us for them make the greatest surprise
Let's make them disbelieve their eyes
My butterflies really hypnotize
When you see my art you'll recognize
What happens when the caterpillar starts to actualize
With my art I begin to romanticize
Let my words make others start to rise
Spirit ignite, release the butterflies!

∞

BUTTERFLIES IN HER MIDST

There were always butterflies in her midst
The butterflies came often and they came swift
The pleasure touched her lightly like mist
She started rotating her wrist
Giving her everything she wished
For pleasures too many to list
Sweetly creating butterflies in her midst
She reached new heights of pleasure I insist
That as she's sleepy and about to drift
To dream state that I be allowed to mix
Her a sexy formula excuse me miss
I'm here to increase your pleasure let me assist
Surrender now there's no way to resist
Let me show you pleasures that didn't exist
Imagining the hotness of our first kiss
There are always butterflies in her midst

∞

Cold Shower

After seeing you I had to take a cold shower
Your beauty makes me shake and want to cower
But I'll be brave and make this happy hour
I'll fertilize your brain like a flower
I'm writing to show you your power
Together our problems and fears we'll devour
You enjoy people with great brainpower
I'm revving up your pleasure button with firepower
You're a unicorn dancing with tremendous horsepower
I'm completely vulnerable with you as I need no manpower
You can do anything with your willpower
I feel like you are a walking sunflower
You are as hot as the sun, now I need another cold shower

CONNECTION

Let's create a truly divine connection
Let's move beyond judgments and imperfections
Let's love so beautifully the world loves a lesson
Let's discover a love beyond expression
Let's make light, let's make a legendary connection
Let's find love that's beyond perception
Let's be each other's cure to depression
Let me give you my full attention
Making you blush, making your face redden
Many compliments in quick succession
Lead us to a new level of connection

∞

Consciousness

What if through divine inspiration and thoughtfulness
I was able to raise the frequency of consciousness
To new heights would I take any consequence
I surrendered all protection and found a bottomless
Well of fresh ideas and with vulnerability could I achieve dominance
Over my ego with great foresight and watchfulness
I treat women like queens with superior opulence
You have taught me self confidence
You taught me the easiest way to get ladies bottomless
Is to tell them they alter you consciousness
You and all your friends are such goddesses
I'm not your secret admirer, I'm willing to express
Ultimate vulnerability I admire your flawlessness
Meaning you are flawesome : fabulously with solemnness
I do declare that you truly alter my consciousness

∞

Conversation

We enjoy the most beautiful conversation
We reflect beauty and increase the amplification
I enjoy watching her pupil dilation
As she's melting and feeling incredible sensations
She receives my authentic application
Of sweetness she's a divine inspiration
We have the most delightful conversation
Pleasure, growth, and respect are our foundation
We are such beautiful reflections our relation
To each other is magic with a little flirtation
We give into pleasure, we give into temptation
Thank you for the most stimulating conversation

∞

CREATIONSHIP

We are evolving and forming a creationship
We're breaking all the rules, going off script
Old paradigms and ideas start to shift
All negative ideas and judgments begin to rip
We encourage each other to rise when we slip
We never cling nor do we try to grip
We are forming a new type of relationship
We are lightmaking, we are a creationship
Our tools we share in order to equip
Ourselves to go further in a spaceship
Let's get outta this world and always lift
Each other up I'm touching her hip
With my mouth and she enjoys my lip
Service all our barriers slowly strip
It's a very unique form of courtship
Let's grow together, let's expand our creationship

∞

Dancing

Me heart feels like it is dancing
When it comes to beauty you give new understanding
To my heart I start planning
New ways to make your heart start dancing
You make me feel like a rockstar so I start jamming
I want to show you light without being demanding
Show you a new definition of feeling outstanding
Let me say you are beyond enchanting
Let my words start inspiring you to start prancing
You're a natural beauty, no need for enchanting
Let me sing you a love song, I'll start by chanting
Things that make you start panting
I'll be totally vulnerable my heart here I am handing
It to you coming in for a smooth landing
You make my heart start expanding
You make me feel alive, like my soul is dancing

Deliciousness

I whisper let me increase your deliciousness
Let me light your fire, let me be your stimulus
More stimulation and much more sinfulness
She enjoyed my treatment of her it was pure deliciousness
She was turned on with pure blissfulness
My hands exciting you with this nimbleness
Let me explore your whole body, I'll be meticulous
In finding your pleasure spots you deserve more deliciousness
I want to drink your juices, you're quite nutritious
You're a beautiful orchid and I'm the sun creating photosynthesis
I want you to feel pleasure describable as ridiculous
Show me your world, I'll share my deliciousness

Divine

When I say that you are divine
What I mean is you are one of a kind
You are absolutely top shelf everything, that's genuine
I feel so blessed to have a muse, mine
I never in my wildest dreams thought she'd find
My artwork beautiful it's really blown my mind
She makes me feel majestically divine
I love to spoil her and encourage her to unwind
All the stars perfectly align
She begins to paint and sip some wine
Thinking wow I really do feel divine

Elegant

Dear you are the most elegant
Lady I am practicing playing and being affectionate
Do you enjoy when someone is really intelligent
I enjoy when someone embodies the word elegant
Which you definitely do I was hesitant
To quit staring you are just so excellent
I swear to me you are heaven sent
But I'm always interested in the elegant excrement
May I melt you some more with great etiquette
You are golden, you are totally in your element
You are the very most elegant

ENDLESS DELIGHT

Tonight it's an honor and pleasure to write
You something that stimulates and excites
You tonight let's have endless delight
I'll say you're amazing and you'll not fight
The feelings, the colors become so bright
This is heavenly and let me please you alright
Your beauty makes me like deer in headlights
My soul was full of kindling, you started to ignite
Passionate words and feelings of endless delight
You love delicious treatment of the polite
Persuasion you are a star, I'll speak of your starlight
I feel like Superman cause you're my kryptonite
Drawing you a bath with lots of candlelight
I'm a dinosaur and you are a meteorite
You rock my world with endless delight

∞

EVOLUTION

She gave me inspiration to start an evolution
She said love wins, love is the solution
Anything other than love is just confusion
I say let's love so big we start a revolution
Let's find true love and clean up the pollution
Loving ourselves greatly is a fantastic evolution
Kindness and respect there's no substitution
No fear, no jealousy, no retribution
Love so energetic it's like electrocution
I slowly surround you in love, it's an infusion
Let's shatter all barriers and illusions
Let's let toxic people go with their delusions
Let's make light and become even greater humans
Let our relationship be a healthy, scared union
Let's support each other fully in our evolution

∞

EXCITEMENT

In your voice I love hearing excitement
I desire to put fire in everything sent
Give you pleasurable sensations most frequent
 Today for you another word present
I'll do anything to hear your excitement
We make light lovingly let's start our ascent
Let's get better every day and never content
Ourselves with anything but the very best I spent
Time today to bring you unlimited excitement
Seeing you makes my mind start to invent
Pleasurable things for you and never relent
I desire to give you pleasure one hundred percent
Then keep going beyond excitement

Fantastic

She deserves to hear that she's fantastic
Together we make art out of the tragic
We choose love, we create magic
Today I'm collecting roses in a basket
I know just how to make her feel fantastic
My belief in her is automatic
She's a timeless beauty, a true classic
When life gets hectic and seems tragic
I'll help you bury all doubt in a casket
Singing your praises is my favorite tactic
I say that you are really fantastic
When you walk you stop traffic
I want to make your heart do gymnastics
She really enjoys my charismatic
Nature together we make art from the traumatic
She deserves romance and I'm very romantic
What's sexier than someone treating you fantastic?
I'm her biggest fan, I'm a fanatic
Daily worship makes her quite orgasmic

FEATHER

I enjoy sharing light there's nothing better
For me than bringing joy and pleasure
To worthy females, it's my favorite endeavor
I am gently touching your heart lightly with a feather
Asking if you know how amazing you are or whether
You'd like me to help you relieve some pressure
On the darkest days with the stormiest weather
Allow me to be your sunshine and rainbows we'll make together
You're my reflection, my greatest treasure
You turn my brain on and make it very clever
Today another gift, another love letter
Today let's experience blessings beyond measure
Let me touch your body all over with a feather
Is that a good touch, does this make you feel better?

∽∞

FIRE

She didn't just survive being in a fire
It made her even hotter that she inspires
Me to write about fiery desire
There are very few things sexier to this writer
Than someone that survives circumstances most dire
Like the Phoenix you rose triumphant from that fire
From the bottom of my heart I really admire
Your magnificent self who cares what was prior
You ignite my brain like a wildfire
There are so very many things about you to admire
I guess I'll start with how you make my entire
Body feel like it's standing next to fire

∞

GENTLENESS

She deserved someone that wasn't venomous
She needed someone with extra gentleness
She was not used to healthy specialness
He treated her with loving elegance
He showed such vulnerability with his eloquence
He warmed her with sweetness and gentleness
His action of love were clear evidence
That he practiced loving her with selflessness
He touched her heart softly whispering you excellence
She learned receiving his sweet helpfulness
He showered her with kisses and preciousness
Se was the first to demonstrate true pleasantness
He stroked her body to ease her restlessness
He was her angel, always loving gentleness

HEARTBREAK

After experiencing so much heartache
Sometimes it may seem difficult to undertake
The experience of receiving like can you forsake
Your old patterns and become more awake
Or are you addicted to the heartbreak
To the yard your delicious milkshake
Brings all the boys but men who make
Habit of kindness and not being a flake
Maybe she could get more than they take
Maybe someone wants a stake
In rocking her world like an earthquake
The difference between real love and fake
Is that love is a choice, not a mistake
Protecting your heart against heartache
Is healing medicine to any heartbreak

HEAVEN

I wonder what it would be like to wake up in heaven
You miss look like Helen
Of Troy I'd burn whole cities, at least seven
And it still wouldn't be as hot as you in a Stetson
I enjoy your style and self-expression
You look hella good is this Armageddon
You are in your own league, you're an eleven
Your style is sharp like a weapon
If life gives you a quick succession
Of opportunities disguised as lemons
I'll holler you're the best blessin
You're the best you, I speak with a pleasant
Tone here's a most interesting question
If you are on Earth, then how hot are the women in heaven
Looking at you feels like heaven every second
Miss do you like where this is headed
Love making you feel honored and respected
This is me totally vulnerable, totally unprotected
You're so heavenly miss, better than heaven!

INFINITELY

We mirror each other's beautiful light infinitely
We bring out the best in each other brilliantly
We share light and reflect magnificently
She makes me feel absolutely heavenly
It's so safe to express ourselves intimately
She makes me feel amazing, like ridiculously
Great is she the most beautiful definitely
I whisper sweet things and my originality
Stems from our light, which shines infinitely

∞

INSECURITIES

Her fire burned away my insecurities
She said if you love me then surely
You intend on loving me purely
Love me brother with purity
Warrior spirit of a Cherokee
Her fierceness brings me clarity
I start to carefully study her rarity
Her mistyped texts full of hilarity
When I love her it's with great clarity
It's an honor to protect my precious carefully
I love her with incredible transparency
I love her a lot apparently
I wrote a book and faced my insecurities
I waited patiently merrily
For the one that heals like therapy
Love me with devotion and maturity
That's how I address all her insecurities

INSPIRATION

Oh I love being a source of inspiration
To you, you deserve incredible sensations
I like being the source of your perspiration
Your beauty creates quite a fixation
Nothing to fix, just pure admiration
You make me feel such uttering this exclamation
You're incredible, you're a beautiful inspiration
Let's make light and let go of all expectations
Let me share my painting and illustrations
She said please me, please provide lubrication
For my heart and soul your art causes liberation
An interesting point of view, my admiration
Of your beauty can I be the source of great titillation
I'll give you all the pleasure with no hesitation
I'd do anything for your pleasure, my true inspiration

∞

INTENSITY

I say fly high with great intensity
Swim in pleasure, get great clarity
Embrace your authentic self, embrace your destiny
Let go of every judgment and negative memory
Shine brighter, sine with intensity
I'll be totally vulnerable and in my vulnerability
I shine my light surely we are heavenly
Let's make beauty that leaves others breathlessly
Let's redefine love and create a legacy
Spirit let me light shine so pleasantly
That it brings us to new levels presently
Today let's shine with blinding intensity!

∞

INTIMIDATING

You ladies all look fierce and intimidating
You are masterpieces that broke out of their framing
Apparently there's a whole bunch of priceless paintings
Is this a fire sale or are they all just flaming
You all look absolutely gorgeous, beyond amazing
In the past your group would have been intimidating
To me but now courage is what you are generating
You all are stunning and absolutely breathtaking
Your beauty was the source of motivating
Me to say I find you all endlessly fascinating
I hope this has succeeded in your spirits raising
I could spend forever and a day praising
All of you, well done ladies, you are all exhilarating
First thought was there's a group that defies taming
They are fun, wild, and really raising
The bar you make my body start levitating
I feel like I'm in heaven, your beauty is intoxicating
To me your group nickname is captivating
You are all very stylish and intimidating

∞

INVITING

What a blessing to be even more inviting
What a blessing to inspire new writing
You inspire hope and that's exciting
I feel like my heart is flying
You inspire me to start trying
New things and new thoughts I'm not riding
A horse because I'm not a knight; I'm describing
How you make me want to strike like lightning
The growth and love in our relationship is highlighting
New opportunities and I am so widely smiling
You touch my heart so much I'm crying
Your willingness to be so open is magically inviting

JUST TURNED ON

I hope to get you to beyond just turned on
You are looking like the Queen of Babylon
Tonight how about I write you a song
Mirror mirror on the wall who's the prettiest fawn
Tell me who would enjoy worship from morning to dawn
I'm slow and gentle now sing along
That guy makes me beyond turned on
I'm in it to win it; it's not a sprint it's a marathon
Whispering in your ear pleasure can be drawn
Out and you aren't lucky and I'm not a leprechaun
I know greatness and when I gaze upon
You're enchanting self I am beyond turned on
You look like you work in a beauty salon
I want to make light to you in the upper echelons
Seeing you makes the most beautiful poetry spawn
I'm willing to do anything to help get you beyond just turned on

∞

Kindness and Openness

She was worthy of kindness and openness
She receives everything she wants nothing less
I am her assistant in relieving stress
We are each other's reflection, we are the best
She deserves my reflection of being a goddess
We play together like it's recess
We inspire new levels of kindness and openness
Her receiving is increasing, it's a process
I speak to her kindly with great finesse
I'm massaging her brain and sweetly caress
Her soul she gives me total access
Miss thank you for allowing me to bless
You with new levels of kindness and openness

∞

LIGHT

She picked up the hummingbird so light
She thought it dead but she might
Bring it back if she believed that right
Now anything was possible and tonight
She was reminded that her life
Had purpose and her body so tight
She breathed deeply and as I write
To her a slow song at midnight
Tonight like the hummingbird you take flight
She's barely hanging on and I light
A fire in her heart being so polite
Massaging her feet under candlelight
I'm her sunshine and she's my moonlight
Safe, gentle sweetness is her kryptonite
I lifted her easily, she's so light

∞

LIGHTMAKING

She is so beautiful and breathtaking
She inspires me to start painting
She sets my heart totally blazing
I whisper things like you are amazing
Let's skip lovemaking and go straight to lightmaking
I'm licking your brain and I'm taking
My time let's discover a new awakening
I'm rubbing you nicely and placing
My hand in yours we are interlacing
Our souls and deliciously lightmaking
I want to give you so much pleasure earthquaking
Let me rock your world like we've been waiting
Patiently to get your addiction blazing
Give into temptation, join me in lightmaking

MELTING

When I see you my heart starts melting
You're so stunning I feel like yelling
But instead of poetry to start telling
You I will accept my fear I am accepting
That taking down all walls can be overwhelming
You are golden and I'm over her smelting
You are so nice and hot that thing you are smelling
Is a passion lit in your soul I'll keep you sweating
You are as hot as lava, my heart keeps melting

∞

MIRROR

I am everything I see in her, I'm her mirror
Her overwhelming external beauty is nothing compared to her inner
Light and my do I admire her delicious figure
Her style is so cutting edge it's killer
Here's an interesting point of view to consider
What if I'm the world's most beautiful mirror
She said your rhymes really deliver
Warmth hey lady has anyone ever said you make them roar
She smiles and says I truly love and adore
Your words, you help lift me up from the floor
She says I empower her and I say you have such allure
Her mind is a treasure and I'd love to explore
How to make her shine brighter from her core
Let's make light and let's keep it pure
Let's be our best reflections, let's be a luxurious mirror

Mistake

She fosters safety and makes my mind awake
She says being vulnerable is no piece of cake
I'm so scared my body starts to shake
I whisper I'm willing to admit any mistake
She's my fortress in the middle of an earthquake
Solid, strong, safe she helps me take
Off my armor and dip in her luscious lake
So refreshing to not worry about if I'll break
She soothes me when I experience heartache
I was in prison to my ego and she helped break
Those chains and together we celebrate
She changes the way that I operate
I'm a human and can admit all my mistakes
A poem to say I really appreciate
You making it safe enough to admit a mistake

∞

Oak Tree

I stand rooted like an old oak tree
You fly wild bird, totally free
I know you'll come back eventually
For my love which to you is heavenly
I'm devoted to treating you pleasantly
Give you the most pleasure you agree
That nothing turns you on like your oak tree
I can see your excitement through your tee
I'm making you hot like a cup of tea
Let me give you pleasure between your knees
It's an honor to serve, it's a pleasure to please
My tongue is so quick, light, and feathery
I'll stand here strongly and wait patiently
My wilds birds always return to their oak tree

ON YOUR MIND

I want to be on your mind
I dream of redefining love and being kind
You're the greatest treasure anyone could ever find
Your beauty is a true gift to mankind
You are so stylish, everything you wear is well designed
Our true purpose in life is to help remind
Others of their inner light I hope you don't mind
If I elaborate on beauty so bright I almost go blind
I want to help you relax and truly unwind
Let me bathe you in luxury and together we'll unbind
Each other and I'm really curious what your behind
Looks like penny for your thoughts, what's on your mind?

∞

ORCHID

She was his exotic, beautiful orchid
Nobody treated her so well, it did
Amazing things to her amid
Her busy life the pressures mounted
She allowed him things most would forbid
He was very safe, very sweet, and timid
Like a cat he kissed her eyelids
She made his imagination run rapid
She makes him the opposite of flaccid
She loves when he shoots his fluid
He regularly waters his orchid

∞

Overflow

Today she needed joy to overflow
So on your marks, ready, set, go
She's moving her body in flow
I whisper you're the best as above so below
She said stand next to my fire and blow
Gently that's very hot whoa
Feelings of pleasure and joy start to overflow
Nothing makes me smile like seeing her glow
Steel sharpens steel, together we grow
Today I just wanted you to know
That thinking of the best way to show
Love is to say you make my heart overflow

∞

PEDESTAL

I don't need to put you on a pedestal
Cause you are already on one you're so special
You make me constantly upgrade my definition of incredible
You really help me bring out my intellectual
Side you make me feel like I'm at a festival
Meaning you make me feel festive and sensual
I want to rise to your level can I stand on a pedestal
With you and play a game of confessional
I do confess you are absolutely delectable
You take me from 3d to fifth dimensional
Can I make you even more meltable
Treat you with great reverence and impeccable
Care you look right home on your pedestal
You light my world on fire I feel it on a skeletal
Level you make my bones explode like a pyrotechnical
Master you rock hard and I love heavy metal
Am I making your body release intoxicating chemicals
You are such an amazing model, total professional
You've created a fire that is unquenchable
I say you are a unicorn, a true mythical
Creature and unicorns belong on a pedestal

∞

PHENOMENAL

I love hearing your voice, it's phenomenal
You are always like you are so adorable
Together for breakfast we eat anything impossible
Hearing nice things about myself in audible
Form is beyond amazing, it's phenomenal
Bringing you intense pleasure I want to be responsible
Treating you lovingly with all honorable
Intentions you bring out my most optimal
Sense of self imagine us in a location that's tropical
Hearing you voice make me feel philosophical
Your cute giggle make me act comical
Let get past reality, the heck with being logical
Let's give you pleasure that's unstoppable
I send you light, hope this makes you feel phenomenal

∞

Pleasurable

I whisper in her ear things most pleasurable
My admiration of her is immeasurable
She can't help but smile, she is unable
To quit smiling my words are unforgettable
Let me bathe you in light most pleasurable
Our friendship creates light it's inevitable
That our spirits will become inseparable
She looks upon me in the most favorable
Light, she screams you are most pleasurable
I make her ignite in ways so memorable

∞

Process

Receiving for us is a new process
It's weird, scary, and uncomfortable but nonetheless
The elephant in the room will be addressed
Total trust, total freedom, open access
Only inspiration, never seeking to possess
After a history of betrayal and distress
We opened ourselves to totally bless
Each other, not perfection but progress
We make it safe to bravely express
Our desire to receive this process
Is working and as we continue experiencing success
We continue to have pleasure beyond excess
Safely we expose the vulnerability, that openness
Joins our souls together in a loving caress
Receiving is a journey, we are trusting the process

∞

QUESTIONS

What if we had fun creating a superior question
Creating light that will never lessen
Would you like to go in a new direction
Admiring your mind instead of your midsection
Can we create a new form of affection
How can I be your secret obsession
Can I increase your pleasure, that's a great question
What about if we have a fun video session
I've got the most interesting confession
Increase your receiving that's a healthy suggestion
Would you help me make a beautiful expression
Would you allow me to help you experience heaven
Would you be willing to be my gorgeous reflection
Can we helpe each other change our perception
Can we help each other redefine perfection
You've got needs and I've got great questions

∞

RECEIVING

On a molecular level you are receiving
Appreciation thanks for treating
Us with your magical presence I enjoyed your dancing and leaning
You make my body feel hot, you are steaming
You move aggressively and you are really heating
Up the vibration of the planet thanks for receiving
For you a word dance a minute of speaking
I want to make your body start shrieking
With joy like this feels like I'm dreaming
Grab your pole and focus on receiving
Pure light from your body giving you just what you are needing
I hope this makes you smile, I hope it leaves you beaming
Thank you for your gifts, I'm so blessed by receiving

∞

REFLECTION

Into me I see you, my intimate reflection
You've got an absolutely perfect midsection
You help create the most beautiful expressions
I desire you pleased beyond measure, it's my obsession
Let's make light brilliantly giving each other a lesson
In pure love let's bask in each other's reflection
You inspire poetry in quick succession
I share with you the most loving affection
Hello beautiful, magnificent reflection
Today I added to your poetry gift collection
You are safe to be completely vulnerable with, I need no protection
You have the most beautiful skin and complexion
Let's be so beautiful we outshine our imperfections
You're the most beautiful, you are my reflection

REQUEST

She said I think I know what you request
I enjoy admiring you, I do confess
If beauty was a crime you'd be forever under arrest
I like your Polaroid pictures the best
I'd do anything to help you feel your best
You are the most stunning, even fully dressed
I'm inspired by beauty and you're above the rest
I'm more interested in your brain than your chest
But why should I bother to repress
My urges to see the most beautiful painting, I'm obsessed
And I never feel guilty making another request

∞

REVEAL

When taking risks I was able to reveal
Many things like layers of an onion I peel
Back more vulnerability here's the deal
Revealing the truth cleared the minefield
The courage to face everything and to feel
Safe enough that I can truly reveal
Anything to you, there's nothing to conceal
Revelations let us find our most ideal
Self; it's worth the risk, every ordeal
We've experienced things so surreal
Truth, honor, and strength are able to unseal
That vulnerability is the ultimate sex appeal
When you trust me fully you reveal
The path to healing, together let's heal

∞

Rockstar

The prettiest lady just called me a rockstar
Inside I'm laughing like that's bizarre
She must be looking in the mirror we both are
Opening to new ideas, you are a jaguar
You are a mermaid that escaped the sandbar
You are luxurious like the finest caviar
You are smoking hot like a Cuban cigar
The best thing about being a rockstar
Is the groupies but I have none only scars
Opening my heart and vulnerability with a crowbar
Being totally vulnerable makes me feel like a rockstar

∞

Rubbing

Allow me to rub you the right way I'm rubbing
Your tired feet and you're quickly becoming
More relaxed it's a pleasure to share loving
Touch let me please you until there's nothing
Left in your head but pleasure let's start rubbing
Each other: oh my it's slowly becoming
Very hot in here, you're so stunning
You're bright as the sun, you're sunning
I beat my soul, firmly I start drumming
Up new ways to please you and I'm rubbing
You so pleasantly you start cupping
Your beautiful breasts saying I'm really loving
Your touch pleasure starts flooding
Your brain and your body are you wanting
Me to go higher is there something else that needs rubbing?

∞

SAFELY

She let me express things candidly and safely
She said say anything, you are free
I said you are like the turquoise sea
You're a wild bird and I'm your oak tree
Safe is the new sexy we both agree
I'm in her flower like a bumblebee
Touching her lightly, almost feathery
We share in a way that nobody
Else does, we share very safely
She said you put a huge emphasis on safety
She asks would you please bend me over your knee
I like being spanked, it fills me with glee
She feels safe exploring her sexuality
She said I love how you never judge me
Together we are creating a new reality
Together we embrace, safe is the new sexy

SAME

Today an attempt to explain
How much you are my butane
You quickly ignite my brain
To write things that make you exclaim
You are my beautiful reflection, we claim
Treasures for source we both gain
Tremendously we never refrain
From sharing light we are the same
We are blending light with the rain
Rainbows flowing through our veins
We surrender to light, releasing any pain
Together there's nothing we can't obtain
You make the craziness seem sane
You are my most stunning reflection, we are the same

SELF-ESTEEM

I focus on building her self-esteem
I know how to make her really beam
She says your focus on what's between
My ears and make love your theme
I desire to make her soul scream
Whispering things most obscene
I make her body start to steam
Showing her pleasure in most extreme
Ways lighting her fire like gasoline
It's sexy when someone builds self-esteem
Tonight her bikini is made of whipped cream
I'm slowly touching her stream
Of consciousness sending a rainbow beam
Through her soul, through her bloodstream
For all per pain I'm the morphine
Safely we focus on being a team
We both give each other wet dreams
Sexily, bravely, boldly building self-esteem

∞

SENSATIONS

She said she'd love to hear another observation
Another point of view to give her incredible sensations
I said can I take you beyond expectations
Can I really open your mind and imagination
Perhaps some fun and innocent flirtations
Together let's make light our favorite creation
Consciousness poetry gives her hot sensations
Together we move to bliss from frustrations
I lift you up, do you enjoy levitation
I empower you with a strong vibration
I could write volumes of all the adoration
I have for you I hope my careful application
Of sweetness gives you increased circulation
I'm so grateful for you, this is my appreciation
Give into feeling amazing, give into temptation
Let me take you beyond exhilaration
Looking at your beauty is a form of meditation
Let's heal everything, love is our medication
I like providing you amazing stimulation
Thanks for helping spur my transformation
You deserve all the very best sensations

∽∞

SENSUAL

She dances slowly, she's so sensual
Releasing everything dancing is so spiritual
Sensual music and dance are medicinal
To her as she shows how bendable
She is a star she's a beautiful pinnacle
Her outfit and makeup we impeccable
He dancing for twenty minutes is unforgettable
She dripping emotions with her dance of sensual
Her dancing is that of a professional
Her passion for dance is unquenchable
Her movements are absolutely delectable
Her dancing is redefining sensual

∞

SOOTHING

To her I am beautiful and soothing
It's nice to have a man not pursuing
An agenda I only care about doing
What's best for everyone I'm grooving
So hard and she appreciates my blooming
I'm her peonies and care about improving
Her mood and her stress starts reducing
Just basking in my energy, it's so soothing
I'm also never bringing her an engagement ring
She deserves a man not bent on seducing
Her she finds me quite amusing
I bathe her in sweetness, it's so soothing

∞

SOPHISTICATED

I don't ask for nudes, I prefer sophisticated
Pictures and you're the most fascinating creature ever created
You are a walking bod of art I waited
My whole life to find something so beautifully sophisticated
Your beauty is truly appreciated
My whole body, it celebrated
When it saw you redefining sophisticated
My eyes are so very captivated
With you your beauty truly fascinated
Me all this poetry and art is motivated
By the way your beauty totally saturated
My mind is ridiculously stimulated
Show me the most intimate, the most sacred
I just can't get enough of you clothed or naked
You're the most beautiful, I feel so creative
When I see you, you're the most sophisticated

∞

SOULGASM

I want to give you your first soulgasm
I'm bringing you pleasure by the wagon
This Eve let me be your Adam
Allow me to be of service madam
I want to pleasure every atom
Of your being your first soulgasm
You're not golden, you're platinum
Allow me to serve with great enthusiasm
I desire to give you pleasure beyond what you fathom
This is how it is going to happen
I'll keep licking you until you spasm
Drenched in sweat, dripping with passion
I'm turning vulnerability into the new fashion
I'm her fire and she's my dragon
Nothing lights her fire like receiving a soulgasm

∞

Spiritual Intellectual Stimulation

What's it like to experience elevation
And what exactly is spiritual intellectual stimulation
Like can I lick your brain without cessation
Can we make light of any situation
Together can we make a beautiful creation
Intelligent stimulation is the foundation
For magnificent, saucy temptation
Just a little bit of flirtation
You fill me up like a gas station
A sexy brain loves mutual admiration
Excellent listening with great concentration
Is vulnerability mixed with strength a winning combination
Oh how you fill me with such fascination
Get someone that shows superior appreciation
For excellent spiritual intellectual stimulation

∞

SUNSHINE

She said good morning sunshine
Vulnerability mixed with being truly kind
Was ultra-sexy and his genuine
Care for his precious feline
Got her feeling great in her mind
His admiration helped her shine
He helped her expand her divine
His treatment of her made her redefine
Sensuality; she loved how he got her to unwind
She bent over and exposed her behind
The moon is out but he's eating sunshine

SUPERMODEL

Is it ever acceptable to ogle
A woman, what if she's a supermodel
You deserve someone really thoughtful
Someone that can make magic from the awful
You on the runway quick grab the nozzle
She's on fire that's why she's a supermodel
She enters and collectively the gasp is audible
She keeps it popping like champagne bottles
Looking at her makes my brain go full throttle
She really excites every single molecule
You really are the hottest supermodel!

∞

SUPERMODELS

I desire to be a super model
Of the right way to admire a supermodel
I wonder how fun it would be to play spin the bottle
With a room full of your friends it really boggles
My brain such prettiness makes me start a novel
I'd like to get their pleasure centers on full throttle
How does it get better than excited supermodels
You all make me philosophical like Aristotle
Treat women like Queens that's the new gospel
Treat women with respect and be courageous, vulnerable, and thoughtful
I want to get biblical but I'm no apostle
I just love the idea of exciting supermodels

∞

THE CRIES

When it got really tough she got the cries
He held her and began to improvise
She had helped him become more wise
When the pain was starting to maximize
He said you know you give me the cries
Too but it's from how you mesmerize
Me the love started to neutralize
Her sadness as he continued to baptize
Her in sweet words surrounding her like butterflies
She wasn't always able to verbalize
How she felt but he gave her the cries
Her tears began to fertilize
The ground and roses started to rise
A beautiful field of roses watered by the cries

TITILLATING

I find your body so very fascinating
I've been over here calculating
The best way to really start stimulating
Oh I know you love when I write titillating
Things your pleasure is motivating
Me to whisper start really concentrating
On my light my fire begins dominating
Your senses your erotic desires are awakening
New sensations my light is intoxicating
Tonight I hope to get you beyond amazing
Is this light pure pleasure, is it titillating?

TOUCHING

I want to make the most light loving
I want you to be unable to quit touching
Yourself like more sweetness and melting
Please say more things that keep me blushing
I am so slow, you love when there's no rushing
With my words I'm slowly brushing
Lightly over your soul I want to tell you something
About being our best selves there's nothing
More inspiring than the thought of you rubbing
Yourself until your body starts gushing
You inspire so much beauty it keeps busting
Out you're a priceless painting and I'm trusting
My heart to say do you feel this, is this touching?

TRUE AND HONORABLE BEING

She calls me a true and honorable human being
I remind her that I'm her reflection she is seeing
There is total respect when we are speaking
Both of us are cautiously believing
In ourselves as true and honorable beings
We bless each other while breathing
In the refreshing delight like we are dreaming
Sincere admiration and vulnerability is freeing
I'm her fireplace when she is freezing
What really lights her fire is reading
How she helps ma become a more true and honorable being

VANITY

I can't help but add to your vanity
If I may speak quite candidly
To the amount of calamity
You cause me, you disturb my sanity
Making my mind race so actively
You're the hottest, it's not vanity
You my dear are a walking fantasy
The source of poetry formed rapidly
Shall I describe how dramatically
You stir my heart or perhaps elaborately
Confess that you're a unique tapestry
You drive me to the brink of insanity
With the way you ooze sensuality
Engulf me in your wanton sexuality
They call you vain, understandably
You're the sexiest in the whole galaxy
It's merely a fact, its' not vanity

WINGS

When she thinks of me her body sings
Our partnership really brings
Out the best in both of us there's nothing
Between us she's a Queen and I'm a King
She's my wingwoman and I'll show her no ring
A black and white world we start coloring
We share a ton, together we can accomplish anything
I'm her guardian angel she's safe under my wing
Let's leap forward, together we spring
She is my personal, private plaything
Together we amass a fortune, we get everything
I lift my friend up, she has her own wings

∞

ZEN

I feel so much gratitude and appreciation
For you my new and fun friend
An acupuncturist that's very Zen
I hope to continually reflect beauty within
Knowing it lifts your spirit and makes you grin
I hope I help make things better than they have been
When I think of where to begin
You move my mind far past sin
Choosing to focus on your brain and chin
Instead of your body or how thin
You are hoping to help us both win
I hope this touches your heart and skin
Knowing you inspired me to pen
Another poem inspiration from you is so Zen

∞

www.ingramcontent.com/pod-product-compliance
Lightning Source LLC
Chambersburg PA
CBHW071953070426
42453CB00012BA/2241